MW01231221

Note to Self...

I AM
ENOUGH

This Journal Belongs to

_____

WE OFTEN COMPARE OURSELVES TO OTHERS AND LEAVE OURSELVES WITH THE NOTION THAT WE ARE NOT ENOUGH. HOWEVER, WE ARE CREATED UNIQUELY, EMBODYING EXACTLY WHAT WE ARE SUPPOSED TO BE. THAT ALONE MAKES US ENOUGH!

THIS JOURNAL WILL HELP YOU DECLARE DAILY THAT YOU ARE ENOUGH. IT WILL GUIDE YOU THROUGH CONFESSING YOUR "ENOUGH-NESS!"

ARE YOU READY TO TAKE THIS 12 WEEK JOURNEY OF REPROGRAMMING YOUR MIND AND EMBRACING JUST HOW AMAZING YOU ARE? YES?! LET'S DO IT!!

EACH DAY YOU WILL JOURNAL SPECIFIC TASKS FOR THE DAY. AT THE END OF EACH WEEK YOU WILL COMPLETE THE WEEK WITH A GUIDED JOURNAL ENTRY THAT WILL HELP YOU CONTINUE ON THE JOURNEY OF EMBRACING YOURSELF AND KNOWING YOU ARE ENOUGH!

-COACH A.D

Date: _____

My "I am Enough" Journal

Read the prompts below and respond by filling each space
provided with images and words that come to mind.

The best things that happened today:	Things I wish I can change about today:
I am proud of myself today because...	I think I still need to work on....

Date: _____

My "I am Enough" Journal

Read the prompts below and respond by filling each space
provided with images and words that come to mind.

The best things that happened today:	Things I wish I can change about today:
I am proud of myself today because...	I think I still need to work on....

Date: _____

My "I am Enough" Journal

Read the prompts below and respond by filling each space
provided with images and words that come to mind.

The best things that happened today:	Things I wish I can change about today:
I am proud of myself today because...	I think I still need to work on....

Date: _____

My "I am Enough" Journal

Read the prompts below and respond by filling each space
provided with images and words that come to mind.

The best things that happened today:	Things I wish I can change about today:
I am proud of myself today because...	I think I still need to work on....

Date: _____

My "I am Enough" Journal

Read the prompts below and respond by filling each space
provided with images and words that come to mind.

The best things that happened today:	Things I wish I can change about today:
I am proud of myself today because...	I think I still need to work on....

Date: _____

My "I am Enough" Journal

Read the prompts below and respond by filling each space
provided with images and words that come to mind.

The best things that
happened today:

Things I wish I can
change about today:

I am proud of myself
today because...

I think I still need
to work on....

Date: _____

My "I am Enough" Journal

Read the prompts below and respond by filling each space
provided with images and words that come to mind.

The best things that happened today:	Things I wish I can change about today:
I am proud of myself today because...	I think I still need to work on....

Journal Writing Exercise

WHY I AM ENOUGH

Date:

Writing a journal helps you recognize your own feelings over certain things or events, no matter how mundane. For this week, write down things that made you feel good and reminded you that you are enough! Record what your positivity goal is for the next week and how you will achieve it.

_____

_____

_____

_____

_____

_____

_____

_____

_____

_____

_____

Date: _____

My "I am Enough" Journal

Read the prompts below and respond by filling each space
provided with images and words that come to mind.

The best things that happened today:	Things I wish I can change about today:
I am proud of myself today because...	I think I still need to work on....

Date: _____

My "I am Enough" Journal

Read the prompts below and respond by filling each space
provided with images and words that come to mind.

The best things that happened today:	Things I wish I can change about today:
I am proud of myself today because...	I think I still need to work on....

Date: _____

My "I am Enough" Journal

Read the prompts below and respond by filling each space
provided with images and words that come to mind.

The best things that
happened today:

Things I wish I can
change about today:

I am proud of myself
today because...

I think I still need
to work on....

Date: _____

My "I am Enough" Journal

Read the prompts below and respond by filling each space
provided with images and words that come to mind.

The best things that happened today:	Things I wish I can change about today:

I am proud of myself today because...	I think I still need to work on....

Date: _____

My "I am Enough" Journal

Read the prompts below and respond by filling each space
provided with images and words that come to mind.

The best things that happened today:	Things I wish I can change about today:
I am proud of myself today because...	I think I still need to work on....

Date: _____

My "I am Enough" Journal

Read the prompts below and respond by filling each space
provided with images and words that come to mind.

The best things that happened today:	Things I wish I can change about today:

I am proud of myself today because...	I think I still need to work on....

Date: _____

My "I am Enough" Journal

Read the prompts below and respond by filling each space
provided with images and words that come to mind.

The best things that
happened today:

Things I wish I can
change about today:

I am proud of myself
today because...

I think I still need
to work on....

Journal Writing Exercise

WHY I AM ENOUGH

Date

Writing a journal helps you record your thoughts and process through them, leaving the positive things in your memory. For this week, write down thoughts that usually make you feel less than. Then process through those and document the positive thoughts that help you remember that you are enough! Record what your positivity goal is for the next week and how you will achieve it.

_____

_____

_____

_____

_____

_____

_____

_____

_____

_____

_____

Date: _____

My "I am Enough" Journal

Read the prompts below and respond by filling each space
provided with images and words that come to mind.

The best things that happened today:	Things I wish I can change about today:
I am proud of myself today because...	I think I still need to work on....

Date: _____

My "I am Enough" Journal

Read the prompts below and respond by filling each space
provided with images and words that come to mind.

The best things that happened today:	Things I wish I can change about today:
I am proud of myself today because...	I think I still need to work on....

Date: _____

My "I am Enough" Journal

Read the prompts below and respond by filling each space
provided with images and words that come to mind.

The best things that
happened today:

Things I wish I can
change about today:

I am proud of myself
today because...

I think I still need
to work on....

Date: _____

My "I am Enough" Journal

Read the prompts below and respond by filling each space
provided with images and words that come to mind.

The best things that
happened today:

Things I wish I can
change about today:

I am proud of myself
today because...

I think I still need
to work on....

Date: _____

My "I am Enough" Journal

Read the prompts below and respond by filling each space
provided with images and words that come to mind.

The best things that happened today:	Things I wish I can change about today:
I am proud of myself today because...	I think I still need to work on....

Date: _____

My "I am Enough" Journal

Read the prompts below and respond by filling each space
provided with images and words that come to mind.

The best things that happened today:	Things I wish I can change about today:

I am proud of myself today because...	I think I still need to work on....

My "I am Enough" Journal

Read the prompts below and respond by filling each space
provided with images and words that come to mind.

The best things that happened today:	Things I wish I can change about today:

I am proud of myself today because...	I think I still need to work on....

Journal Writing Exercise

WHY I AM ENOUGH

Date

_____

_____

_____

_____

_____

_____

_____

_____

_____

_____

_____

Date: _____

My "I am Enough" Journal

Read the prompts below and respond by filling each space
provided with images and words that come to mind.

The best things that happened today:	**Things I wish I can change about today:**
I am proud of myself today because...	**I think I still need to work on....**

Date: _____

My "I am Enough" Journal

Read the prompts below and respond by filling each space
provided with images and words that come to mind.

The best things that happened today:	Things I wish I can change about today:
I am proud of myself today because...	I think I still need to work on....

Date: _____

My "I am Enough" Journal

Read the prompts below and respond by filling each space
provided with images and words that come to mind.

The best things that happened today:	Things I wish I can change about today:
I am proud of myself today because...	I think I still need to work on....

Date: _____

My "I am Enough" Journal

Read the prompts below and respond by filling each space
provided with images and words that come to mind.

The best things that
happened today:

Things I wish I can
change about today:

I am proud of myself
today because...

I think I still need
to work on....

Date: _____

My "I am Enough" Journal

Read the prompts below and respond by filling each space
provided with images and words that come to mind.

The best things that happened today:	Things I wish I can change about today:
I am proud of myself today because...	I think I still need to work on....

Date: _____

My "I am Enough" Journal

Read the prompts below and respond by filling each space
provided with images and words that come to mind.

The best things that happened today:	Things I wish I can change about today:
I am proud of myself today because...	I think I still need to work on....

Date: _____

My "I am Enough" Journal

Read the prompts below and respond by filling each space
provided with images and words that come to mind.

The best things that
happened today:

Things I wish I can
change about today:

I am proud of myself
today because...

I think I still need
to work on....

Journal Writing Exercise

WHY I AM ENOUGH

Date

Writing a journal helps you remember the compliments and well wishes you have received. For this week, write down something that someone may have said that boosted your confidence and reminded you that you are enough! Record what your positivity goal is for the next week and how you will achieve it.

_____

_____

_____

_____

_____

_____

_____

_____

_____

_____

_____

Date: _____

My "I am Enough" Journal

Read the prompts below and respond by filling each space
provided with images and words that come to mind.

The best things that happened today:	Things I wish I can change about today:
I am proud of myself today because...	I think I still need to work on....

Date: _____

My "I am Enough" Journal

Read the prompts below and respond by filling each space
provided with images and words that come to mind.

The best things that happened today:	Things I wish I can change about today:

I am proud of myself today because...	I think I still need to work on....

Date: _____

My "I am Enough" Journal

Read the prompts below and respond by filling each space
provided with images and words that come to mind.

The best things that happened today:	Things I wish I can change about today:

I am proud of myself today because...	I think I still need to work on....

Date: _____

My "I am Enough" Journal

Read the prompts below and respond by filling each space
provided with images and words that come to mind.

The best things that
happened today:

Things I wish I can
change about today:

I am proud of myself
today because...

I think I still need
to work on....

Date: _____

My "I am Enough" Journal

Read the prompts below and respond by filling each space
provided with images and words that come to mind.

The best things that happened today:	Things I wish I can change about today:
I am proud of myself today because...	I think I still need to work on....

Date: _____

My "I am Enough" Journal

Read the prompts below and respond by filling each space
provided with images and words that come to mind.

The best things that happened today:	Things I wish I can change about today:

I am proud of myself today because...	I think I still need to work on....

Date: _____

My "I am Enough" Journal

Read the prompts below and respond by filling each space
provided with images and words that come to mind.

The best things that
happened today:

Things I wish I can
change about today:

I am proud of myself
today because...

I think I still need
to work on....

Journal Writing Exercise

WHY I AM ENOUGH

Date

Writing a journal helps you emotional health. For this week, write down the emotions that you felt and highlight the ones that made you see that you are enough! Record what your positivity goal is for the next week and how you will achieve it.

_____

_____

_____

_____

_____

_____

_____

_____

_____

_____

_____

Date: _____

My "I am Enough" Journal

Read the prompts below and respond by filling each space
provided with images and words that come to mind.

The best things that happened today:	Things I wish I can change about today:

I am proud of myself today because...	I think I still need to work on....

Date: _____

My "I am Enough" Journal

Read the prompts below and respond by filling each space
provided with images and words that come to mind.

The best things that happened today:	Things I wish I can change about today:
I am proud of myself today because...	I think I still need to work on....

Date: _____

My "I am Enough" Journal

Read the prompts below and respond by filling each space
provided with images and words that come to mind.

The best things that happened today:	Things I wish I can change about today:

I am proud of myself today because...	I think I still need to work on....

Date: _____

My "I am Enough" Journal

Read the prompts below and respond by filling each space
provided with images and words that come to mind.

The best things that happened today:	Things I wish I can change about today:
I am proud of myself today because...	I think I still need to work on....

Date: _____

My "I am Enough" Journal

Read the prompts below and respond by filling each space
provided with images and words that come to mind.

The best things that happened today:	Things I wish I can change about today:
I am proud of myself today because...	I think I still need to work on....

Date: _____

My "I am Enough" Journal

Read the prompts below and respond by filling each space
provided with images and words that come to mind.

The best things that happened today:	Things I wish I can change about today:

I am proud of myself today because...	I think I still need to work on....

Date: _____

My "I am Enough" Journal

Read the prompts below and respond by filling each space
provided with images and words that come to mind.

The best things that happened today:	Things I wish I can change about today:
I am proud of myself today because...	I think I still need to work on....

Journal Writing Exercise

WHY I AM ENOUGH

Date

Writing a journal helps you boost your mood. For this week, write down a moment that your mood could have been compromised but you were determined to remember that you are enough! Record what your positivity goal is for the next week and how you will achieve it.

_____

_____

_____

_____

_____

_____

_____

_____

_____

_____

_____

_____

Date: _____

My "I am Enough" Journal

Read the prompts below and respond by filling each space
provided with images and words that come to mind.

The best things that
happened today:

Things I wish I can
change about today:

I am proud of myself
today because...

I think I still need
to work on....

Date: _____

My "I am Enough" Journal

Read the prompts below and respond by filling each space
provided with images and words that come to mind.

The best things that happened today:	Things I wish I can change about today:
I am proud of myself today because...	I think I still need to work on....

Date: _____

My "I am Enough" Journal

Read the prompts below and respond by filling each space
provided with images and words that come to mind.

The best things that happened today:	Things I wish I can change about today:
I am proud of myself today because...	I think I still need to work on....

Date: _____

My "I am Enough" Journal

Read the prompts below and respond by filling each space
provided with images and words that come to mind.

The best things that
happened today:

Things I wish I can
change about today:

I am proud of myself
today because...

I think I still need
to work on....

Date: _____

My "I am Enough" Journal

Read the prompts below and respond by filling each space
provided with images and words that come to mind.

The best things that happened today:	Things I wish I can change about today:
I am proud of myself today because...	I think I still need to work on....

Date: _____

My "I am Enough" Journal

Read the prompts below and respond by filling each space
provided with images and words that come to mind.

The best things that happened today:	Things I wish I can change about today:
I am proud of myself today because...	I think I still need to work on....

Date: _____

My "I am Enough" Journal

Read the prompts below and respond by filling each space
provided with images and words that come to mind.

The best things that happened today:	Things I wish I can change about today:
I am proud of myself today because...	I think I still need to work on....

Journal Writing Exercise

WHY I AM ENOUGH

Date

Writing a journal can be a stress reducer. For this week, write down things that could have been stressful but your "enough-ness" helped get you through it! Record what your positivity goal is for the next week and how you will achieve it.

_____

_____

_____

_____

_____

_____

_____

_____

_____

_____

_____

Date: _____

My "I am Enough" Journal

Read the prompts below and respond by filling each space
provided with images and words that come to mind.

The best things that happened today:	Things I wish I can change about today:
I am proud of myself today because...	I think I still need to work on....

Date: _____

My "I am Enough" Journal

Read the prompts below and respond by filling each space
provided with images and words that come to mind.

The best things that happened today:	Things I wish I can change about today:

I am proud of myself today because...	I think I still need to work on....

Date: _____

My "I am Enough" Journal

Read the prompts below and respond by filling each space
provided with images and words that come to mind.

The best things that happened today:	Things I wish I can change about today:
I am proud of myself today because...	I think I still need to work on....

Date: _____

My "I am Enough" Journal

Read the prompts below and respond by filling each space
provided with images and words that come to mind.

The best things that
happened today:

Things I wish I can
change about today:

I am proud of myself
today because...

I think I still need
to work on....

Date: _____

My "I am Enough" Journal

Read the prompts below and respond by filling each space
provided with images and words that come to mind.

The best things that happened today:	Things I wish I can change about today:

I am proud of myself today because...	I think I still need to work on....

Date: _____

My "I am Enough" Journal

Read the prompts below and respond by filling each space
provided with images and words that come to mind.

The best things that happened today:	Things I wish I can change about today:
I am proud of myself today because...	I think I still need to work on....

Date: _____

My "I am Enough" Journal

Read the prompts below and respond by filling each space
provided with images and words that come to mind.

The best things that
happened today:

Things I wish I can
change about today:

I am proud of myself
today because...

I think I still need
to work on....

Journal Writing Exercise

WHY I AM ENOUGH

Date

As you close out week 8, the number of completeness, take a look back at your past 7 entries. For this week, write down noticeable signs of growth and new habits of acknowldgeing that you are enough! Record what your positivity goal is for the next week and how you will achieve it.

_____

_____

_____

_____

_____

_____

_____

_____

_____

_____

_____

Date: _____

My "I am Enough" Journal

Read the prompts below and respond by filling each space
provided with images and words that come to mind.

The best things that happened today:	Things I wish I can change about today:

I am proud of myself today because...	I think I still need to work on....

Date: _____

My "I am Enough" Journal

Read the prompts below and respond by filling each space
provided with images and words that come to mind.

The best things that
happened today:

Things I wish I can
change about today:

I am proud of myself
today because...

I think I still need
to work on....

Date: _____

My "I am Enough" Journal

Read the prompts below and respond by filling each space
provided with images and words that come to mind.

The best things that happened today:	Things I wish I can change about today:
I am proud of myself today because...	I think I still need to work on....

Date: _____

My "I am Enough" Journal

Read the prompts below and respond by filling each space
provided with images and words that come to mind.

The best things that
happened today:

Things I wish I can
change about today:

I am proud of myself
today because...

I think I still need
to work on....

Date: _____

My "I am Enough" Journal

Read the prompts below and respond by filling each space
provided with images and words that come to mind.

The best things that
happened today:

Things I wish I can
change about today:

I am proud of myself
today because...

I think I still need
to work on....

Date: _____

My "I am Enough" Journal

Read the prompts below and respond by filling each space provided with images and words that come to mind.

The best things that happened today:	Things I wish I can change about today:
I am proud of myself today because...	I think I still need to work on....

Date: _____

My "I am Enough" Journal

Read the prompts below and respond by filling each space
provided with images and words that come to mind.

The best things that happened today:	Things I wish I can change about today:
I am proud of myself today because...	I think I still need to work on....

Journal Writing Exercise

WHY I AM ENOUGH

Date

Writing a journal helps you express gratitude. For this week, write down
things about yourself that you are thankful for. Document how these things
remind you that you are enough! Record what your positivity goal is for the
next week and how you will achieve it.

_____

_____

_____

_____

_____

_____

_____

_____

_____

_____

_____

Date: _____

My "I am Enough" Journal

Read the prompts below and respond by filling each space
provided with images and words that come to mind.

The best things that happened today:	Things I wish I can change about today:
I am proud of myself today because...	I think I still need to work on....

Date: _____

My "I am Enough" Journal

Read the prompts below and respond by filling each space
provided with images and words that come to mind.

The best things that
happened today:

Things I wish I can
change about today:

I am proud of myself
today because...

I think I still need
to work on....

Date: _____

My "I am Enough" Journal

Read the prompts below and respond by filling each space
provided with images and words that come to mind.

The best things that
happened today:

Things I wish I can
change about today:

I am proud of myself
today because...

I think I still need
to work on....

Date: _____

My "I am Enough" Journal

Read the prompts below and respond by filling each space
provided with images and words that come to mind.

The best things that
happened today:

Things I wish I can
change about today:

I am proud of myself
today because...

I think I still need
to work on....

Date: _____

My "I am Enough" Journal

Read the prompts below and respond by filling each space
provided with images and words that come to mind.

The best things that happened today:	Things I wish I can change about today:
I am proud of myself today because...	I think I still need to work on....

Date: _____

My "I am Enough" Journal

Read the prompts below and respond by filling each space
provided with images and words that come to mind.

The best things that happened today:	Things I wish I can change about today:
I am proud of myself today because...	I think I still need to work on....

Date: _____

My "I am Enough" Journal

Read the prompts below and respond by filling each space
provided with images and words that come to mind.

The best things that happened today:	Things I wish I can change about today:
I am proud of myself today because...	I think I still need to work on....

Journal Writing Exercise

WHY I AM ENOUGH

Date

Writing a journal helps you learn from your own experiences. For this week, write down experiences of the week. Document the positive highlights that helped you remember that you are enough! Record what your positivity goal is for the next week and how you will achieve it.

_____

_____

_____

_____

_____

_____

_____

_____

_____

_____

_____

Date: _____

My "I am Enough" Journal

Read the prompts below and respond by filling each space
provided with images and words that come to mind.

The best things that
happened today:

Things I wish I can
change about today:

I am proud of myself
today because...

I think I still need
to work on....

Date: _____

My "I am Enough" Journal

Read the prompts below and respond by filling each space
provided with images and words that come to mind.

The best things that
happened today:

Things I wish I can
change about today:

I am proud of myself
today because...

I think I still need
to work on....

Date: _____

My "I am Enough" Journal

Read the prompts below and respond by filling each space
provided with images and words that come to mind.

The best things that
happened today:

Things I wish I can
change about today:

I am proud of myself
today because...

I think I still need
to work on....

Date: _____

My "I am Enough" Journal

Read the prompts below and respond by filling each space
provided with images and words that come to mind.

The best things that happened today:	Things I wish I can change about today:

I am proud of myself today because...	I think I still need to work on....

Date: _____

My "I am Enough" Journal

Read the prompts below and respond by filling each space
provided with images and words that come to mind.

The best things that happened today:	Things I wish I can change about today:
I am proud of myself today because...	I think I still need to work on....

Date: _____

My "I am Enough" Journal

Read the prompts below and respond by filling each space
provided with images and words that come to mind.

The best things that happened today:	Things I wish I can change about today:
I am proud of myself today because...	I think I still need to work on....

Date: _____

My "I am Enough" Journal

Read the prompts below and respond by filling each space
provided with images and words that come to mind.

The best things that happened today:	Things I wish I can change about today:

I am proud of myself today because...	I think I still need to work on....

Journal Writing Exercise

WHY I AM ENOUGH

Date

Writing a journal helps your progression toward accomplishing goals. For this week, write down goals that you may have. Acknowledge your awesome level of "enough-ness" and how it will help you accomplish this goal. Record what your positivity goal is for the next week and how you will achieve it.

_____

_____

_____

_____

_____

_____

_____

_____

_____

_____

_____

_____

_____

Date: _____

My "I am Enough" Journal

Read the prompts below and respond by filling each space
provided with images and words that come to mind.

The best things that happened today:	Things I wish I can change about today:
I am proud of myself today because...	I think I still need to work on....

Date: _____

My "I am Enough" Journal

Read the prompts below and respond by filling each space
provided with images and words that come to mind.

The best things that happened today:	Things I wish I can change about today:
I am proud of myself today because...	I think I still need to work on....

Date: _____

My "I am Enough" Journal

Read the prompts below and respond by filling each space
provided with images and words that come to mind.

The best things that
happened today:

Things I wish I can
change about today:

I am proud of myself
today because...

I think I still need
to work on....

Date: _____

My "I am Enough" Journal

Read the prompts below and respond by filling each space
provided with images and words that come to mind.

The best things that happened today:	Things I wish I can change about today:
I am proud of myself today because...	I think I still need to work on....

Date: _____

My "I am Enough" Journal

Read the prompts below and respond by filling each space
provided with images and words that come to mind.

The best things that
happened today:

Things I wish I can
change about today:

I am proud of myself
today because...

I think I still need
to work on....

Date: _____

My "I am Enough" Journal

Read the prompts below and respond by filling each space provided with images and words that come to mind.

The best things that
happened today:

Things I wish I can
change about today:

I am proud of myself
today because...

I think I still need
to work on....

Date: _____

My "I am Enough" Journal

Read the prompts below and respond by filling each space
provided with images and words that come to mind.

The best things that happened today:	Things I wish I can change about today:
I am proud of myself today because...	I think I still need to work on....

Journal Writing Exercise

WHY I AM ENOUGH

Date

Writing a journal helps you discover your voice and puts you in touch with
your authentic self. For this week, write down ways that this journey has
helped you discover your voice. Record how this process has helped you
walk confidently and embrace your "enough-ness!"

_____

_____

_____

_____

_____

_____

_____

_____

_____

_____

_____

Made in the USA
Columbia, SC
07 January 2025

49167288R00057